MW00333190

Glimpses of My Life and Career and The People Who Made Them:

A Palestinian Story

BY

ADEL K. AFIFI, M.D., M.S.

The picture on the front cover titled 'Serenity' was painted by Adel Afifi on June 27, 2019, in memory of Larry Anna Afifi.

©2020 Iowa City, Iowa, United States of America
ISBN: 978-0-578-63770-9
LCCN:2020901065

Glimpses of My Life and Career and The People Who Made Them

IN GRATITUDE TO

MY PARENTS
who appreciated the value of education

MY BROTHERS, SISTERS IN-LAW, AND SISTER
Ramez, Fouzieh, Nabih, Hassana, and Nabiha
and
Larry Anna (Teta)
whose love and support were boundless

OUR TREASURES
Rima, Walid, Tammy, Loulwa, Leah, Tala, Leila, Rania
and
the late infant Mohammad

AND OUR LIFELONG FRIENDS

50th ANNIVERSARY, GRUIN RESTAURANT, BEIRUT
FAMILY & FRIENDS

Glimpses of My Life and Career and The People Who Made Them

Table of Contents

Glimpses of My Life and Career and The People Who Made Them

ACKNOWLEDGMENT

THIS NARRATIVE could not have been possible without my cherished colleagues at the American University of Beirut Faculty of Medicine Drs. Kamal Badr and Nabil Kronfol, as well as Abdo Jurjus who provided the photos of my mentors at the American University of Beirut archives.

Credit goes to members of my family who took time from their busy schedules to edit the manuscript and make valuable suggestions in text and style. My daughter Rima, son Walid, daughter-in-law Tammy, and grandchildren Loulwa, Leah, and Tala. The inserting of photos in the text would not have been possible without the expertise of Rima, Walid, and Dr. Zuhair Ballas.

Special credit goes to Chris Dickey for editing and Robyn Hepker for designing of the book.

To all, my deep gratitude.

Glimpses of My Life and Career and The People Who Made Them

MEMOIRS

*"Memoirs are a kind of archeological dig to help the memoirist see him
or herself for what he or she is, in terms of who you have become, and
of the experiences and the people that have helped shape your life."*

Hemley. R.
A Field Guide for Immersion Writing, *2012, p. 58*

Thus, the narrative that follows is not a detailed memoir, rather a glimpse
of experiences and the recognition of the people who helped shape my life
and career.

PREAMBLE

THIS IS A PERSONAL STORY of dispossession and displacement that fell upon a whole nation in 1948; and the struggle to keep moving forward against all odds.

If there is a lesson in this narrative, it is that faith, family and goodness will triumph over bigotry and oppression.

This is a story of a generation, who witnessed the rise of Arab nationalism, and the hope for a united secular single Arab State, the decline of that hope, and the rise, in frustration, of religious extremism.

A generation described by Edward Said, the renowned Palestinian author, as one for whom "living war, the threat of war, and the loss from war have become a way of life."

A generation that lived the "Nakba" and the massacres of Deir-Yassin, Qibya, Qana, Kafr Qasim, Jenin, Nahr el Barid, Ibrahimi mosque, Dawaymeh, Sabra and Shatila camps, among others; the defeat of Arab armies by Israel; the rise and fall of Palestinian armed resistance (Fedayeen); Black September; the Lebanese Civil War, and the dragging of the Palestinian resistance into it; the siege of an Arab capital (Beirut) by Israel; the first and second intifadas in Palestine; the Oslo accord; two Camps David (Egyptian and Palestinian); emergence of the Palestinian Authority (PA); split of Fateh and Hamas; the Separation of Gaza from the West Bank and East Jerusalem; the Siege of and repeated onslaught on Gaza by the Israelis, to mention only a few of the tragedies that have befallen the Palestinians.

Throughout, Palestinians remain stateless, and suffer the void of not belonging, best described by Edward Said "no home, no road , no passport, a community scattered and discontinuous, for which all events are accidents, and where no straight line leads from home to birthplace to school to maturity."

Perpetrators of the Nakba counted on the second generation of Palestinians to forget. On the contrary, the image of Palestine and of Palestinians remain vivid in the minds and hearts of children and grandchildren of those affected by the Nakba. Some of the grandchildren, including mine, wrote about the

"Key" symbol of the lost home; others continue to mass together to celebrate "Land Day" and the "Right of Return" incurring in the process injuries and death. Palestinians under occupation and in the Diaspora have kept the issue of Palestine alive in academic institutions, societies, the BDS movement, writing books and lecturing. In doing so, Palestinian children will for many more generations keep the memory of Palestine alive. In his acceptance speech of an Honorary Doctorate from the American University of Beirut (AUB) in June 2012, Munib Masri, prominent Palestinian philanthropist, ended his speech by "The Old will continue the struggle, and the young will not forget."

INTRODUCTION

AS I REFLECT ON MY LIFE and career, I recognize the large number of people who made it possible for me to achieve what I did.

First and foremost, my family, my late parents, Kassem Afifi and Zeinab Akki, my late brothers, Ramez and Nabih, and their families, and my late sister Nabiha. Their boundless love, sacrifices, and belief in the value of education made it possible for me to stay the course.

Support, encouragement, and sacrifice of my wife, Larry Anna, our children Rima and Walid, and their children Loulwa, Leah, Tala, Leila and Rania, made it possible to achieve what I did academically and socially.

Their support and that of many others of our friends and acquaintances became critical following the Nakba (Catastrophe) that befell the Palestinians between November 1947 and May 1948, when 750,000 to one million Palestinians, including my family, were abruptly dispossessed from their homes and properties, and dispersed in the neighboring Arab countries and beyond.

Overnight, my family became refugees in Lebanon with no access to their property and income. All of a sudden, they found themselves in a foreign land, known only by their name and refugee status. Gone was the power of their family name and the reputation of their forebears.

*"We dwell in many homes on earth,
the dearest is the place of birth"*
W.M. Cortas
A World I Loved, *2009*

Glimpses of My Life and Career and The People Who Made Them

FORMATIVE YEARS: GROWING UP IN AKKA (1930-1946)

I WAS FORTUNATE TO GROW UP in the small town of Akka, Palestine in a family of good means under the guidance of loving parents, two older brothers, Ramez and Nabih, and a sister, Nabiha, who unfortunately passed away at the age of fourteen from bacterial meningitis just before the era of penicillin. Also living with us was our nanny, Ratiba (Dada), a loving and caring person.

We lived in a beautiful house with a veranda overlooking the Mediterranean Sea.

Akka is an ancient city dating back to over 4,000 years. It is mentioned in the Torah and in the Bible Book of Judges. Over the years, Akka was known by several names, Akko, Akki, Ptolomius, Ptolemeus, Colonia Claudia Felix, Jean d'Arc, Acre, and Akri. The most commonly used names are Akka (Arabic), Acre (British), and Akko (Hebrew). The name Akka dates back to 636 AD when it was occupied by the Arabs.

Being a main seaport in the Eastern Mediterranean, Akka was a favorite stop over for pilgrimages from Europe on their way to the holy places in Jerusalem and beyond. Among such people was Apostle Paul, the famous Muslim traveler Ibn Jubair, and the famous Muslim physician Muwaffaq el Din al Baghdadi.

In his book "Embers and Ashes", Dr. Hisham Sharabi described Akka as the most beautiful city in the world.

Laurence Olifant described Akka "of all towns along the Syrian shore, there is no other town where history's so full of events such as Acre, and there is no other town whose influence on the whole country was so grand."

One of my most memorable places growing up was the Afifi Garden, in an-Nahr village, about 10 miles north of Akka. The Garden and the adjacent mansion were built by Mohammed Afifi, my father's uncle, for the family. We routinely spent family time in it during vacations and holidays. In addition, visiting dignitaries were allowed to have receptions in the Garden and Baha'u' Allah, leader of the Baha'i religion, used the Garden as a meditation area. The Garden was destroyed, along with the village, when Zionist militants invaded.

Intuitive Discovery or Commonly Known Habit

One of the glimpses of my early childhood was having to drink a teacup full of strong Turkish coffee every morning before going to school. The rest of the family drank the classical small cup (demicup) of the same coffee.

I do not know why I had to go through this daily exercise when no one else in the family did, nor was I told why!

I do not recall how I reacted to this routine other than I remember taking the coffee cup out of the house to the covered stairs to drink it, possibly a sign of protest?

In view of what we know today about the effect of stimulants on hyperactive children, it is conceivable that I was a hyperactive child calmed by strong coffee stimulant.

Whether this relation of coffee and hyperactivity was a commonly known practice at that time or was an intuitive discovery by my mother, I cannot tell. However, knowing the amount of coffee that mother consumed daily, and her acute sense of observation and inquisitiveness, it is not inconceivable that she may have given some to me and noted the calming effect.

If the latter were the case, it is unfortunate that she did not publish her findings and receive credit for this important discovery.

Early Education

For pre-school, I enrolled in a private catholic pre-school run by Sister Martha. The school was the first private pre-school in Palestine.

For my elementary and two years of my secondary education, I enrolled in public schools whose curricula were rigorous following the English system of education.

Two teachers in the secondary school left an impact on me: The poet Nasir el Isa, and the Arabist Rafiq Lababidi who instilled in me awareness of my national identity, love of Palestine, the threat of Zionism, and the beauty and richness of the Arabic language.

The rest of my secondary education was completed in the Prep School of the American University of Beirut, Lebanon.

At the Prep School, Professor Shafiq Jeha instilled in me the love of history, which I still cherish and write about.

ADEL AND NABIHA IN ACRE HOME
AGE 4 AND 8, 1934

Professor Shafiq Jeha

COLLEGE YEARS
AND THE IMPACT OF THE NAKBA

LIKE ALL PALESTINIAN STUDENTS of my age, I started my college year in 1947 in financial jeopardy.

Fortunately, AUB had begun a Palestinian Students Loan Fund to make it possible for Palestinian students to begin or to continue their college education.

While this fund covered part of the tuition fees, it did not cover all fees. The rest were provided by selling some of my mother's jewelry, and by borrowing from family friends, notably the Amin family from Akka, and Mrs. Irani, my mother's ex-seamstress.

With support provided by AUB and friends, I was able to complete four years of college and receive the B.Sc. degree.

Glimpses of My Life and Career and The People Who Made Them

THE AUB COLLEGE YEARS:
A RETROSPECTIVE

AS I LOOK BACK at my AUB College years, I recognize the important role it played in shaping who I became.

AUB not only provided its students with the necessary knowledge and skills to succeed in life, but more importantly, with a sense of who we are, a sense of belonging to our culture and heritage, and a determination to leave the world a better place.

It also provided mentors who instilled in us the spirit of inquiry, and the excitement of scientific discovery.

AUB provided opportunities for us to get involved in several kinds of societies and clubs (Urwat al Wuthqa, Civic Welfare League, and Student Council, among others). Those experiences were central in developing my national awareness, civic responsibility, value of collective wisdom, and civility of discourse. In addition, AUB allowed us to meet and blend with people from varying nationalities, ethnic origins, cultures, and religious affiliations. These affordances were central in nurturing life- long friendships. Among these friendships are:

My classmate Dr. Nakhleh Zarzar who, upon hearing my intent to seek a scholarship from the Royal Jordanian Army Medical Services in return for twenty years commitment to serve in the Royal Medical Services, visited my family during my absence in Jordan to offer instead to advance me the needed funds.

My very close friend, counselor and life-long brother, Dr. Samih Alami who was there when I needed him, who taught me a lot about philanthropy, and who during the Civil War in Lebanon, would not go to bed before ensuring the necessary fuel, medical supplies and food for the University Hospital.

My mentor, Dr. Afif Muffarej, who insisted on being present in the operating room to assist when our son Walid was injured by a shrapnel during the Lebanese civil war.

MEDICAL SCHOOL
(1951–1957)

MEDICAL SCHOOL WAS NOT my personal choice. It was my mother's wish that one of her children become a doctor, and another of her children become a pharmacist.

This desire was not unique to my mother. It was common among mothers in the Middle East to take pride in being referred to as "Um al Hakim" the Doctor's Mother. It turns out that this favored title of Arab mothers originated in Hebrew culture where the doctor was next in rank only to the Rabbi.

Thus, my oldest brother Ramez elected to go into pharmacy at AUB; my next older brother Nabih elected to go into medical school at AUB, and I decided to pursue a career in Arabic Culture and literature.

This plan however changed abruptly when my brother Nabih fainted when he visited the anatomy dissection room prior to applying to medical school. Instead of medicine, he registered to study education and political sciences.

To please my mother, I changed my choice of study. I enrolled in the medical school instead of Arabic culture and language; a decision I never regretted. I continued to pursue Arabic culture and language as a hobby.

FINANCIAL CHALLENGES:
MEDICAL SCHOOL DETOUR – PART I (1951-1952)

The financial support provided by the AUB Palestinian Loan Fund and from other sources described above ceased once I received my first college degree, the B.Sc., which included the first year of medical school.

There were no apparent sources of funds for me to continue my medical education. So, I resorted to request the medical school to allow me to take one-year leave of absence to teach full time at the Prep School, the University high school. Thanks to the Dean of the medical school, Dr. Joe McDonald, and the Associate Dean Dr. Musa Ghantus, my request was approved.

Dean Dr. Joe McDonald   *Associate Dean Dr. Musa Ghantus*

Prof William Shanklin

MEDICAL SCHOOL DETOUR – PART II (1952-1954)

At the end of a year teaching at the Prep School, I was still short of funds to return to medical school, and again asked the Dean for an extension of my leave from medical school for another year.

The Dean was not in favor of having me away from medical school for another year.

Instead, the Dean along with the Associate Dean Dr. Musa Ghantus, and the chair of the

Department of Histology and Neuroanatomy Dr. William Shanklin, made an arrangement for me (first in the history of the medical school) to do my second year of medicine in two years instead of one. By this arrangement, I would be employed in the Department of Histology and Neuroanatomy for two years (1952-1954) during which time I would complete the curriculum of the second year of medical school, and at the same time earn an income and gain experience in research under the well-known neuroanatomist Dr. Shanklin.

TEACHING ENGLISH GRAMMAR IN PATHOLOGY

A pathology course in the second year of medical school consisted of acquainting students with the tissue and organ pathology that may explain the disease. That was not all we were taught in the course that Dr. Nimr Tuqan gave to my class. Dr. Tuqan was a brilliant physician and pathologist who also was endowed with a sense of humor that endeared him to his friends and the politicians of the country.

During one of the sessions of the pathology laboratory, Dr. Tuqan distributed to each student a microscope glass slide to study and report to him what they saw in the slide. He stressed that he was not interested in detailed description of what is in the slide, rather he wanted a diagnosis. It did not take much examination of the slide to make the diagnosis. There were liver tissues and cancer cells, easy diagnosis!

When we returned the slides to Dr. Tuqan, those students who made the diagnosis 'cancer in the liver' got a grade of 'A' while those who made the diagnosis 'cancer of the liver' failed the test. The lesson that Dr. Tuqan wanted to convey to us is the difference between a diagnosis of commission implied in the use of the word 'of the liver' and the diagnosis of omission implied by the use of the word 'in the liver.'

This is a lesson I have not forgotten, and it made me a better user of words to convey a diagnosis.

Light at The End of The Tunnel:
UNRWA Scholarship (1954)

Before the end of 1954, my family and I started looking for other options of financial assistance to make it possible for me to complete the remaining years of medical education.

One option was to contact AUB Vice President, Dr. Fuad Sarruf who was in charge of scholarships to needy students. Access to Dr. Sarruf was through a distinguished Lebanese woman, Mrs. Nimat Kronful, mother of one of my students, Nabil Kronful, and an acquaintance of my brother Ramez.

Another option we explored was the Jordanian Royal Army Medical Corps who granted fellowships to study medicine in England in return for serving in the Corps for twenty years. Access to that selection committee was through Mayor Dihmis, father of my classmate Carlos Dihmis and mayor of a town near Bethlehem in the Occupied Palestinian Territories

Ms. Nimat Kronful

Dr. Fuad Sarruf

Thus, I flew from Beirut to Jerusalem and from there drove to the Mayor's house with the help of a pharmacist in Jerusalem, Abu el Said, classmate of my brother Ramez.

The visit with the Mayor went very well. He assured me of his support for my application. From there I drove to Amman for the interview with the selection committee of the Royal Jordanian Medical Corps.

Not known to me during my absence in Jordan, a class mate of mine in AUB medical school, Nakhleh Zarzar, visited my family in Beirut to offer to loan me the funds needed to complete my years in medical school to avoid having to commit my services to the Army Medical Corps for the stipulated twenty years.

Nakhleh came from Bethlehem in Palestine. They had made their wealth before the Nakba working in South America.

The third option we explored was with the United Nations Relief and Works Agency (UNRWA) Scholarship Committee.

As we were contemplating the different options, I learned that the application to the United Nations Relief and Works Agency (UNRWA) for Palestinian refugees in Lebanon, had been approved. That was the light at the end of the tunnel. The fellowship provided tuition, books, living expenses and instruments for the three remaining years with no conditions attached.

Although my good academic record and motivation helped secure the UNRWA scholarship, I am certain that my brother Nabih's senior position in the Education Department of UNRWA helped secure the fellowship. Credit is also due the Mr. Mahmoud Amin, family friend from Akka and with high contacts at UNRWA, whose recommendation must have carried its weight among UNRWA decision makers.

THE CLINICAL YEARS (1954-1957)

With the financial burden behind, I was able to devote time to medical students' activities which culminated, during my last year in medical school, with my election to president of the Medical Students Society (MSS).

With an enthusiastic team of Society members, we were able that year to sponsor the following activities:

1. Monthly free clinic in a house provided by the Rasamneh family in Deir Qubel, a village about ten kilometers south of Beirut.

2. Smallpox vaccination drive in the Quarantina area, a poor area of Beirut.

Medical Students Society (MSS) cabinet, 1956, Jiddu president.

3. MSS Anniversary Celebration.

4. Annual Medical School Students (MSS) Show.

5. Annual MSS Yearbook.

6. Annual popular MSS Dinner and Dance, proceeds of which went to support needy patients.

7. Active participation in the organization of the Middle East Medical Assembly, an annual gathering of medical practitioners in the Middle East to catch up on

recent developments in the medical profession. Speakers were usually from AUB faculty as well as invitees from Europe and the USA.

One of my achievements as President of the MSS was to submit an application to the Alpha Omega Alpha (AOA) Medical Honor Society in the USA, for membership. The AOA Medical Honor Society recognizes scholarly achievements and the professional qualities that make an outstanding physician including leadership, service, and professionalism. The application from our medical school was accepted by AOA. Several students and faculty in the AUB medical school are currently active members of AOA.

In retrospect, I believe my intense involvement in students' life throughout my college years and in particular during my leadership of the Medical Students Society was a major reason for being awarded the prestigious Penrose Award at graduation from Medical School. The Award was named after Stephen Penrose, President of AUB who died from massive heart attack while working in his office at AUB. The Award was given to one graduate from each of the four colleges of the University on the basis of scholarship, character, leadership qualities, and contribution to university life.

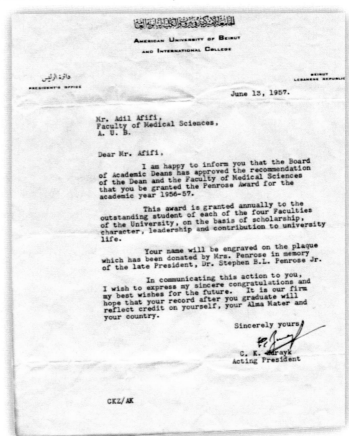

Penrose Award letter

GRADUATION AND INDUCTION INTO AUB MEDICAL ALUMNI (JUNE 1957)

The day finally came when I could assume the title of Doctor of Medicine. My mother attended the graduation, but not my father. He was at home, sick. My two brothers were out of the country in Iraq.

Immediately following the graduation ceremony, I went home to show my proud father the diploma and the Penrose Award. I was happy that he and my

MD Graduating Class, 1957

mother lived long enough to witness the day and the fruits of their sacrifices and love.

A few days after graduation, as customary at AUB, the graduating medical students were inducted into the AUB Medical Alumni Association. For this ceremony, Dr. Jacob Thaddeus, Secretary General of the Medical Alumni, introduced each of the graduates by a poem describing the particular graduate. When my turn came to be introduced, he said "Next comes the debonair Afifi, the MSS President, in love affairs al'Americaine, an expert so confident." Referring to my dating Larry Anna Patten, my girlfriend at the time and later my wife.

MEDICAL SCHOOL YEARS: A RETROSPECTIVE

As I reflect on the contributions of the many great mentors in the medical school, four stand out without whom I could not possibly have completed my medical education: Dean Dr. Joe McDonald, Associate Dean Dr. Musa Ghantus, Chair of the Department of Histology and Neuroanatomy Dr. William Shanklin, and Chairman of the Department of Internal Medicine Dr. Riad Tabbara. Together, these four designed an educational program, unprecedented in the history of the medical school, which made it possible for me to complete my medical education and graduate with the Penrose Award.

A medical education at AUB instilled in me the conviction that medicine is first and foremost a "calling" not a business, which it seems to be drifting into nowadays.

Clinical mentors preached, in words and deeds, the importance of empathy, honesty, humanism, and total commitment to the patient and his or her family in the practice of the profession. Some like Drs. Riad Tabbara, Munib Shahid, Fuad Sabra, and Shafiq Haddad were the first to teach us about humanism in medicine years before my mentor, Dr. Arnold Gold (Professor of Child Neurology at the New York Neurological Institute), popularized an award for humanistic medicine in the USA.

Holding on to these noble principles made of me a better person and physician.

Dr. Riad Tabbara

Dr. Fuad Sabra

Dr. Munib Shahid

Dr. Shafiq Haddad

SAUDI ARABIA AND ARAMCO: TALE OF THE AMERICAN MARINE AND THE SAUDI SHEPHERD (1957–1959)

FOLLOWING MY GRADUATION from medical school, in 1957, my first two priorities were:

1. Help my brothers in support of my parent's living expenses.

2. Pay back AUB and family friends' loans.

Like many of my Palestinian colleagues, I took a detour from graduate medical education to work at the medical department of the Arabian American Oil Company (ARAMCO) in Saudi Arabia.

Besides providing the needed funds, working in ARAMCO helped me sharpen my clinical skills, learn how to play bridge, meet very fine people from all over the world, experience Saudi culture, and the beauty of the Arabian desert.

I also learned that the camel has the right of way on highways and violators who cause injury to the camel would serve jail time until the camel is fully recovered.

Although alcohol sales and use were prohibited in Saudi Arabia, it was available and used in private homes of American employees. I came head on with this dilemma when an inebriated US marine was brought one evening to the ARAMCO hospital with several bruises and cuts after driving his motorcycle through a company of sheep and the shepherd, killing a number of sheep and their Saudi shepherd.

The shepherd was declared dead on arrival to the hospital. The marine was taken to the operating room to attend to his bruises and cuts.

This medical decision on my part was interpreted by the Saudi police as neglecting the Saudi shepherd in order to attend to the American marine. Consequently, the Saudi authorities would have blocked my travels out of

Saudi Arabia and confiscated my passport, were it not for the weight that ARAMCO attorneys held in the Saudi legal system. They resolved the issue in my favor.

Camel stop in Saudi Arabia

Oasis in Saudi Arabia

RETURN TO AUB
(1959-1961)

AFTER I LEFT ARAMCO, I was invited by the Dean of the AUB medical school, Dr. Joe McDonald, to join the faculty in the medical school to teach and do research in the department of anatomy.

As much as I welcomed this gesture from the Dean, I was torn between committing myself to a life-long career of teaching and research at AUB or pursue residency training.

Again, Drs. Joe McDonald and Ghantus came to my rescue. They suggested I join the faculty of the medical school for two years, split between teaching, research, and residency training.

At the end of the two years, my interest in teaching and research were enhanced and I developed special interest in neuroscience and a career in academic medicine.

Cutting our wedding cake

A big bonus of the two years, however, was meeting Larry Anna Patten who, on June 17, 1960, became my wife. We were fortunate that both sides of our family appreciated the value of diversity, accepting to bless our courtship and marriage.

We first met on the third floor of the internal medicine building one evening when she was the nurse in charge, and I was the intern in charge. The floor that evening was not too busy, and we had a group of cordial residents, students, and nurses.

Somehow the discussion among the group touched on coffee in different parts of the world, and Larry Anna asked me if I would show her how to fix Arabic coffee, which I was delighted to do since I was by that time a coffee-holic.

That was the beginning of a very happy courtship that culminated in a very happy 56-year marriage, two children, Rima and Walid, and six grandchildren Loulwa, Leah, Mohammad, Tala, Leila and Rania.

As the end of the two years of teaching, research and residency training was near to end, I shared my decision about my future with Dean McDonald, Associate Dean Dr. Ghantus, Chair of Internal Medicine Dr. Riad Tabbara, chair of Neurology Dr. Fuad Sabra, and chair of neuroanatomy and histology Dr. William Shanklin. All were supportive and pledged to have a post for me in the medical school after finishing my training in the US.

After exploring centers in the USA known for their excellence in clinical neurology and neuroscience research, they worked out a plan for me to go to the University of Iowa in Iowa City to complete four years of training in clinical neurology and research in neuroanatomy.

Glimpses of My Life and Career and The People Who Made Them

The University of Iowa: Post Doctoral and Residency Training — Home Away From Home (1961–1964)

Cottage on the River (1961–1962)

Before arriving in Iowa City, we were informed by the University of Iowa that we were assigned married housing in a compound on campus known as "The Cottages by the River." We were very excited by the news for we never before had the opportunity to live close to rivers or oceans.

We arrived in Iowa City on a gloomy September day and went straight to the only hotel in the city at that time, The Hotel Jefferson, to rest for the night before moving to our "Cottage by the River."

The following day was again a dreary cold cloudy day. We headed to our assigned cottage and almost collapsed when we entered the so-called "cottage."

The "cottage" was indeed by the Iowa River, one of many cottages purchased by the University from remnants of Army tin barracks of the Second World War!

Cottage by the River, Iowa City

It had an ice box for food refrigeration. Heating was provided by a gas heater in the center of the living room. It was scantly furnished.

The Iowa City winter was harsh that year, and many a night we had ice on the inside walls of the living room.

We tried to move out to an apartment in town. The owner of the only available apartment in town asked for a pledge not to have children. So, we had to manage in the "Cottage by the River" for the rest of the year before we moved to a nearby apartment for the rest of our stay.

But what made up for the un-pleasant accommodation of the "cottage," were the neighbors of the compound, young married students; and the staff of the Department of Anatomy who went out of their way to make our stay as comfortable as humanly possible.

NEUROANATOMY FELLOWSHIP (1961-1962)

Bill Kaelber and Adel

I was fortunate at the University of Iowa to work with a superb group. My immediate mentor was Dr. William (Bill) Kaelber who introduced me to modern experimental neuroanatomy which I later introduced to the AUB research endeavor. Research collaboration between the two of us continued after I returned to Beirut and during two sabbatical years, I spent in Iowa City.

Dr. Rex Ingram

Dr. Rex Ingram, chair of the department of anatomy, was a gracious human being and a giant in his field of neuroanatomy. He would stop by my office every morning to ask how my research was going and offer any help he could provide.

My research project, and subsequently my Masters in Neuroanatomy thesis, was focused on the neural connections of the Substantia Nigra of the brain after placing stereotactic lesions in it using a modern stereotactic instrument designed by Dr. Ingram, a copy of which was given free to me when I finished my training to use in my research in Beirut.

When I returned to Beirut, I continued my research on the substantia nigra with financial support from the USA National Institute of Health (NIH).

THE CAMEL BRAIN

Dr. Donald Brown

The year of fellowship gave me the opportunity to meet and work with two wonderful persons who became life-long friends. William (Bill) Osborne, chair of radiation research, became interested in work I did and published on the sub-commissural organ of the camel brain when I was in AUB. The sub-commissural organ at that time was believed to be the center for aldosterone, the hormone that controlled sodium and potassium metabolism. Dr. Osborne wanted to duplicate my results by use of radiation to ablate the area and study the effect of that ablation on electrolytes metabolism.

The other life-long friend was Donald Brown, who at that time was a student in the combined MD/MS program interested in studying the sub-commissural organ. He approached Dr. Ingram seeking a research advisor from the Anatomy Department. Dr. Ingram suggested that I be his advisor since I was the only member of the department at that time who was familiar with the sub-commissural organ, having published on the sub-commissural organ in the camel. The interaction with Don continued beyond the mentorship period since Don became my cardiologist when we returned to Iowa City permanently.

THE JAGUARUNDI AND JAGUAR

The year of the fellowship was not only hard work in teaching and research but included some fun and hilarious days.

Dr. John Way, a neuroanatomist in the department of anatomy was obsessed with having a Jaguar brand car but could not find one in town that he could afford until he read in the city paper about a university student wanting to sell her Jaguarundi.

John called the student and before very long was at her dorm room negotiating to buy her long-awaited Jaguar car. To John's disappointment, the for-sale Jaguar was not a car but a pet animal, a Jaguarundi.

Being a fan of comparative neuroanatomy, John bought the animal and housed it in the animal quarters of the Anatomy Department, where it remained for several years until Bill Kaelber and I decided to study the brain of the Jaguarundi in search of its unique ability for night vision.

John Way's yard, Iowa City

Neurology Residency (1962–1964)

The residency in neurology was very rigorous and clinically oriented as was planned. Historically, the Department of neurology at the University of Iowa was the third department to be established in the USA after Harvard and Columbia Universities. It celebrated its centennial year in August 2019.

Dr. Adolph Sahs

Residents had open access to all the faculty and met with Dr. Adolph (Adie) Sahs, the chairman, daily including on weekends to discuss and manage cases. It was possible for so-inclined residents to indulge in clinical and basic research. Other faculty included Associate Chair Dr. Maurice Van Allen and Dr. Arthur Benton.

Dr. Maurice Van Allen

While in residency training, I was enchanted by the electron microscopic images presented during neuropathology rounds and decided to explore and learn the technique. I was encouraged to pursue my interest by Dr. Fernando Aleu, Professor of neuropathology and electron-microscopy, who took me under his wings, for which I will remain forever grateful. I will also forever be grateful to Fernando for introducing me to Aqua Lavanda, a very fine Spanish after shave lotion, for which he was the sole agent in the USA.

Dr. Arthur Benton

Glimpses of My Life and Career and The People Who Made Them

Genuine Observation or Pitfall of The Novice?

As I became more and more confident in the use of the electron microscope, I was asked by Dr. Hans Zellweger, Professor of Pediatrics to look at muscle biopsies of some of his patients with a variety of muscular disorders. One family of such patients had two varieties of a type of muscle disorders known as congenital myopathies.

The mother had central core disease, while the daughter had nemaline (rod) myopathy. This diversity in diagnosis was intriguing to Dr. Zellweger who asked me to look at the two biopsies from the mother and daughter using the electron microscope.

It turned out from electron microscopic imaging that the abnormalities at the center of the muscle fibers (central core) and those under the sarcolemma (nemaline) in both the mother and daughter were of the same consistency suggesting that the two disorders, central core and nemaline myopathy were indeed two variants of the same pathologic abnormality, not two different disorders. When my findings were published it raised debates about the authenticity of my findings, some believed they were artifacts, others agreed with the findings as genuine.

The debate went on until a well- known and highly respected scientist at NIH examined a few of my tissue samples from the mother and daughter and confirmed my findings as genuine.

Farewell to Iowa Neurology: Nurse's Letter (1964)

"There is a neuro resident of whom we're very fond,
He came to be among us from far off Lebanon,
He livens up our clinic, and I'm sure that you'll agree
One of his greatest assets is his unbounded energy,
He greets us in the morning with his cheery, sweet "Hello"
And he really works us until it's time to go!
New York has beckoned to him and from us he'll soon depart,
Never to be forgotten, for he's won our very hearts."

THE NEW YORK NEUROLOGICAL INSTITUTE: (1964–1965) FRIENDS OF FUAD SABRA ARE MY FRIENDS

$\curlyvee$

SHORTLY BEFORE COMPLETING my neurology residency at the University of Iowa, I received a letter from Dr. Fuad Sabra, chair of neurology at AUB asking me to spend a year at the New York Neurological Institute before returning to AUB. Dr. Sabra had trained at the Institute and was impressed by the quality of training there.

During a visit to New York to attend a meeting, I passed by the NY Institute of Neurology to inquire about the likelihood of admitting me to the Institute. The lady that received me informed me that applicants to the Institute apply several years before starting and not few months as in my case! I asked her if I could talk to Dr. Houston Merritt, the Institute Director, who came out of his office to invite me in.

When he asked me for the reason I wanted to come to the Institute, I told him that I was instructed by Dr. Fuad Sabra, the chair of neurology at AUB to spend time in the Institute before returning to Beirut.

He then asked me if I knew Dr. Sabra, which I answered in the affirmative. He then said "My son, friends of Fuad Sabra are my friends. When do you want to start?"

And this was the beginning of a year plus of training at the New York Neurological Institute devoted to clinical training, research, and teaching.

The faculty members of the Institute were experts in their particular field of interest in neurology and were very supportive.

The opportunity to participate in the teaching of neuroanatomy with the legendary teacher Dr. Malcolm Carpenter was of great importance to me as I learned how clinical neuroanatomy ought to be taught, a method I carried with me to AUB and was the basis of a book on "Functional Neuroanatomy" which I wrote with Dr. Ronald Bergman as co-author.

One of the good aspects of training at the New York Institute of Neurology was opportunities for the faculty and residents to meet and interact in settings outside the patient-oriented settings on the wards. Two such activities remain vivid in my memory of training at the Institute: The Marchiafava- Bignami, and the Guillain -Barre Clubs.

THE MARCHIAFAVA-BIGNAMI CLUB

During my first week in the Institute, I read on the bulletin board the schedule of conferences and meetings during the week. Among the scheduled clubs was the Marchiafava-Bignami Club on Friday at 5:00 PM in the quarters of the residents in the Institute. I took note of that announcement assuming that it was a discussion of the rare disease in Italians who drink contaminated wine. Especially so that the chief resident Dr. Leon Prockop kept reminding me not to miss that particular club meeting.

It was to my surprise when I arrived at the assigned place that the Marchiafava–Bignami club was a get together sponsored by the Institute faculty to entertain the residents and nurses of the Institute every last Friday of the month. Drinks and food were served in an amiable atmosphere where the faculty and residents could talk about anything except neurology!

Peggy Copple at meeting in Oregon

Members of the Guillain-Barre Club, Afifi Apt., NYC

The Guillain-Barre Club

Similarly the Guillain-Barre Club was organized by the chief resident in child neurology, Dr. Peggy Copple, to celebrate the discharge of a child with Guillain- Barre who developed all the complications of the disease but recovered from all of them thanks to the continuous 24-hour attention provided by the residents and nurses assigned to her at the Institute. The club met in a bar near the Institute on the third Friday of the month.

Farewell Gift

When it became time for me to return to AUB, I was surprised to know that Dr. Merritt, Director of the Institute, provided support to me and Larry Anna to spend time in Europe on our way to Beirut. A noble gesture reflecting the character of the man.

Glimpses of My Life and Career and The People Who Made Them

RETURN TO LEBANON: FACULTY YEARS AT AUB

(1965-1984)

THE OLD DAYS CONTRACTUAL AGREEMENTS

In comparison to today's elaborate process of applications and interviews, my application to return to AUB was very simple.

Prior to completing my training, I wrote to Dr. Fuad Sabra, chair of the Department of Neurology at AUB, informing him that I completed my training and asked him what I should do next to apply to return to AUB.

In response to my letter, he answered on a non-official AUB stationary "You have an appointment at AUB from now and forever." No official contract, no salary quote, no definition of responsibility, no conditions.

Based on this non-official piece of stationary, I returned to AUB.

It was simply a contractual transaction based solely on Dr. Sabra's faith in me, and my trust in his words.

AND IT WORKED!

AND SURVIVED!

A RETROSPECTIVE

My return to Beirut and AUB first and foremost brought happiness to my family, but especially to my mother who thought I may never go back to Beirut.

Polyphasia Politica, Agraphia Scientifica

Shortly after I returned to AUB, Dr. Fuad Sabra, Chair of Neurology at AUB, invited me to lunch at the AUB faculty club.

At lunch, he told me that his invitation was to alert me not to fall victim to a disease that some of my colleagues who returned to AUB after training in the USA catch. A disease he called "Polyphasia Politica, Agraphia Scientifica," which he further explained to mean "getting involved in politics of the country and neglecting scientific pursuits."

A sample of Dr. Sabra's known subtle humor.

Ascending the Academic Ladder

Like every new appointee, I started the academic ladder in a low academic rank of instructor (1965), and climbed in rank with accelerated promotion time profile to assistant professor (1966), associate professor with tenure (1969), professor (1974), department chair (1969-1984), and associate dean (1969-1978).

By design, my clinical and administrative responsibilities were such that they would not negatively impact teaching and research. On the contrary, in some instances, clinical encounters enhanced my teaching and research.

Building a New Department

When Dr. Musa Ghantus retired from chairmanship of the department of gross anatomy, I was asked to amalgamate that department with the department of histology and neuroanatomy and chair the new department which I proposed to call the Department of Human Morphology. With time and the recruitment of a highly qualified group of faculty members and assistants, we were able to transform the department into a vibrant entity in teaching and research, to develop, jointly with the other basic medical science department, graduate masters and doctoral programs, and attract funds from the Diana Tamari Sabbagh Foundation to support qualified candidates to the doctoral program, as well as visiting faculty members from the region. The new department, with its full complement of faculty, staff and students was a busy hub of teaching and research.

Adel as Chairman of the new Dept. of Human Morphology

A unique feature of the department faculty and related programs was inclusion of faculty from St. Joseph Medical School in teaching joint courses. The other unprecedented feature was attracting research-oriented practitioners in Beirut to donate time toward research and teaching in courses offered by the new department. One example was the generous donation of time by a successful dentist in private practice, Dr. Joseph Tamari, toward teaching and research in the department. These experiences helped expose students to a unique set of perspectives not typically part of medical school systems at the time.

THE FIRST WORKSHOP ON TEACHING OF ANATOMICAL SCIENCES IN THE MIDDLE EAST (FEBRUARY 5-9, 1975)

In 1975, the newly established Department of Human Morphology at AUB co-sponsored with the Association of Medical Schools in the Middle East a workshop on the teaching of anatomical sciences in the Middle East. International experts in medical education were invited to participate in the workshop. Sixty invitees from the medical schools in the region attended the meeting. The proceedings of the workshop were subsequently published in a book in 1977. Credit is due to the faculty and staff of the Department, to the Lebanese air carrier Middle East Airlines for attending to the details of the meeting, and to Mrs. Phyllis Bergman for editing the book.

Attendees at the First Workshop on the Teaching of Anatomical Sciences in the Middle East, AUB, February 5–9, 1975.

First row, left to right: Drs. Nuwayri-Salti, Lufti, Mahran, Ford, Nassif, Ghantus, Dowidar, Ali, Asper, Moffat, El-Rakhawy, Etemady, Malaty, Afifi.

Second row left to right: Harper, Khachierian, Mire-Salman, Negm, Bauhuth, Atoub, Al-Abbas, Nour-Et-Din, El-Ershi, Fatani, Chaudhry, Azad, Vardar, El-Samanoudy, Sa'di, Yassen, Ibrahim.

Third row, left to right: Jurjus, Nahabedian, El-Winn, Tasieruth, Bergman, Messayeh, Mena, Hakime, Telkian, Saa'deh, Helmy, Azzawi, Osman, De-Wit

TEACHING

At the time of my return to AUB, the College of Medicine was embarking on re-design of the basic medical science curriculum to make it more integrated and clinically oriented.

Working with Dr. Suhayl Jabbur, neurophysiologist, the two of us re-designed the medical neuroscience course integrating neuroanatomy with neurophysiology and some clinical neurology. The re-designed course was very well received by students and was copied in other basic medical science courses.

UNEXPECTED VISITOR IN MY FIRST LECTURE AT AUB

The topic of my first lecture to medical students at AUB was about split brain preparation. What I did not expect was for Dean Joe McDonald, a plastic surgeon but also neuroanatomist, to attend the lecture. He sat in the last row of the lecture room.

Because of the tenseness of the situation, I made an error in drawing, on the black board, the direction of the line in the corpus callosum splitting the two hemispheres. At the end of the lecture, Dean McDonald came to me, and in a very kind tone of voice let me know how much he enjoyed my first lecture but called my attention to the error I committed in the direction of the line splitting the two hemispheres. It was a comment I appreciated then, thanked him for it, and will never forget.

One aspect of my lectures that endeared me to students was the humorous attention-grabbing introduction I typically gave to my lectures. In subsequent years when I happened to meet ex-students during flights or in faraway places, they still remembered those introductions!

STUDENTS

Looking back at those happy and fulfilling years of teaching at AUB, I feel a sense of pride at having contributed, in a small way, to the career of some of my students who went on to become successful in their professional careers, neurological or other fields. They are too many to name, and I am reluctant to start naming them for fear my failing memory will forget many others.

RESEARCH

Throughout my career, my research activity was collaborative and addressed issues relevant to conditions encountered in clinical practice.

The fact that I returned to AUB with funding from the National Institute of Health (NIH), the major research donor in the USA, coupled with the availability of research space provided by AUB, helped me continue developing an active research program upon my return.

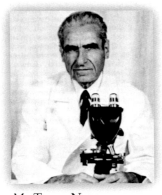

Mr. Tamer Nassar

In addition, the successful early start and continued success of my research program could not have been possible without the expertise and commitments of research assistants Tamer Nassar (supervising and training junior assistants), Nadia Bahuth (neural tracts tracing techniques and electron microscopy), JoAnne Myer (electron microscopy), Winny Kazan (computer specialist), Jihad Hawi (technician), Artemis Kocherian (research assistant), and Shake Tomayan (secretary).

As my research progressed, it was supported by the Lebanese Council of Scientific Research for the rest of my stay at AUB. The Counsel also supported a number of my trips to the USA to attend meetings and collaborate in research with co-investigators. For this I owe Dr. Mustafa Soufi, Director of the Council, gratitude for his support and trust.

Diagnostic and Research Centers

ELECTROMYOGRAPHY AND NERVE CONDUCTION

It was apparent upon my return to AUB that expertise and equipment for electro-physiology was needed. The temporary facility to do electromyography established in the physiology department was inadequate and unreliable. It was not placed in a shielded room and frequently one would encounter external interruptions from broadcasting stations in town.

With the support of Dr. Fuad Sabra, and the technical expertise of Mr. George Tomeh, a properly designed, shielded, and equipped electromyography unit was established in the hospital. My training in electromyography, both in Iowa and at the New York Institute of Neurology, came handy in running the unit.

ELECTRON MICROSCOPY

As mentioned earlier, during my training at the University of Iowa, I was enchanted with, and learned how to use the electron microscope as a diagnostic and research tool in neurological disorders and particularly in neuromuscular disorders, which was one of my major clinical and research interests.

While still in the US, I made my interest in electron microscopy known to both the President of AUB Dr. Samuel Kirkwood, the Dean of the medical school, Dr. Raif Nassif, and the Chair of Neurology, Dr. Fuad Sabra. All were supportive and budgeted funds for the purchase of an electron microscope to be placed in the department of anatomy.

"SEARCH FOR KNOWLEDGE EVEN IF IN CHINA"

This is an Arabic saying encouraging people to seek knowledge even if they have to travel as far as China.

In preparation for the arrival of the microscope and the design of the electron microscopy space, I did not need to travel to China. Baltimore was closer. At Johns Hopkins University was an internationally known electron-microscopy expert, and funds were available from the Commonwealth Foundation for AUB to send their faculty to Hopkins for training.

Dr. Ronald Bergman

I travelled to Hopkins to work with Dr. Ronald Bergman and at the same time, visit the company, in New Jersey, from which AUB purchased the electron microscope.

The visit to Baltimore, and work with Dr. Ronald Bergman, were God-sent. Dr. Bergman was the ideal mentor and became a life -long friend who later moved from Hopkins to AUB. He and I co-authored a number of books and other publications. His commitment to AUB and Lebanon were such that even though many of the foreign faculty left AUB and Lebanon during the Lebanese civil war, Ron and his family stayed.

Decoration ceremony for Dr. Bergman

Collaborative efforts with Dr. Ron Bergman

Celebrating with Dr. Nassif (Dean)

Even injury to one of their sons by shrapnel did not dissuade them from staying. In response to a suggestion that he consider leaving Lebanon, he said "I have seen this country on its hay days, I am not about to abandon it during its dark days"

His contributions to the educational system in Lebanon was recognized by the Minister of Health of Lebanon who honored him by bestowing on him the Lebanese Order of Education at a reception for the purpose held in our home in Beirut. Similarly, the chairman of the Palestine Liberation Organization honored him by presenting him a beautiful artifact made in Bethlehem.

Over time, the electron microscopy unit at AUB became a leading center for training in electron microscopy of individuals from medical schools in the Region.

THE MOST EXPENSIVE CONSULTATION

The civil war in Lebanon lasted between 1975 and 1990. In 1982, Israel launched an offensive in Beirut.

In July 1982, during a bad evening in Beirut, rockets were exchanged between east and west Beirut. A telephone call received by Dr. Samih Alami from the secretary of a well-to-do philanthropist, asking for the "doctors" to come and check him. She was concerned that he has not been able to sleep for several nights, and he was traveling the following day for an important meeting and needed to be awake and alert at the meeting. The "doctors" she was referring to were the cardiologist Dr. Fuad Jubran, Dr. Samih Alami, clinical pathologist, and myself, the neurologist. The three of us were referred to as a trio.

Upon arrival to where he was, we were informed that he was asleep. Nevertheless, the secretary woke him up and brought him to the room where we were waiting. The three of us in turn examined him thoroughly and could not find anything of concern. We assured him and her of his sound health status, and recommended that he takes a sleeping pill to help him sleep soundly before travelling to the meeting.

As we were getting ready to leave the reception room, Dr. Alami asked a favor from the philanthropist. A school in Beirut was in the red for the year due partly to admitting needy Palestinian students for free. Dr. Alami asked if he would cover the school deficit of $60,000.

The philanthropist, with a smile, obliged and looked at the three of us saying "This is the most expensive consultation I have ever had to pay. I was asleep, you woke me up, and you put me back to sleep, for $60,000."

THE TWO BRAINS!

On one of my visits to the State of Qatar to examine the mother of the Ruler's wife, I met the foreign minister of Qatar who came to the hospital to visit her. He asked me to explain what was happening in Lebanon, referring to the ongoing civil war.

Not to indulge in endless dialogue about the matter, I told him "I wish I knew what is going on and what is driving the conflict"

In response, he asked me "Doctor, how many brains does a person have?"

To which I answered "to my knowledge your highness only one brain"

He retorted correcting me "No, we have two brains, each one of us, the God given one we receive at birth and cannot change; and the acquired brain that we acquire from going to universities and become learned people." Then he went on to say, "If the people with the second brain rule Lebanon, the civil war and conflict will cease immediately".

ADMINISTRATION

MEET THE ASSOCIATE DEAN

It was a beautiful spring day in Beirut, I had just finished my work in the office and I was stepping out of the door of Van Dyke building when I came across the Medical School Dean, Dr. Raif Nassif, chatting with the chairs of the different departments of the medical school. He called me to join them and introduced me to them, "meet the new Associate Dean of the School of Medicine." The announcement was news to me and to them. In response to the news, one of the chairs commented "Here we lose a scholar to administration."

My tenure in administration of the school consumed much of my time but was very gratifying in the opportunity it provided me to interact with the Dean, chairs of departments, students and trainees. I owe gratitude to

Dr. Raif Nassif who coached me during my tenure and to Leila Bitar, the assigned secretary from the Dean's office who organized my busy schedule of appointments, and correspondence.

One of my achievements in the Dean's office was to eliminate the age limit of 18 years for admission to medicine. When I assumed the position of Associate Dean for Academic Affairs in 1969, it was a written rule of AUB that students applying to enroll in the medical school should be over 18 years at the time of admission. One of the students (N.N.) applying for admission for medical school in 1972 was 18 years old. Accordingly, the University registrar turned down her application.

The Dean of the medical school, Dr. Raif Nassif and I agreed that this restriction on age for admission was neither scientific nor fair. I was asked to challenge the registrar's decision. I presented the case to the medical school faculty who unanimously approved a motion to delete the age for admission from requirements. I then had to take the case to the Faculty of Arts and Sciences for approval. Again, the motion was overwhelmingly approved, and this young bright female student was admitted to the medical school and performed very well and graduated on time with her class.

In July 1978, after nine years of service as associate dean, I submitted my resignation to devote more time to my academic pursuits.

THE PRESIDENT WANTS YOU TO CALL HER

During the civil war days in Lebanon, in March mid '70s, the President of AUB (an American) had to leave the country for safety reasons. A local interim president was in charge. The interim president at the time was Mrs. Salwa Said. I had known Salwa and her husband Fuad well as I treated their son when he was suffering from a serious neurologic problem.

"Adel, I have to travel to New York to attend the AUB Board of Trustees. Will you act for me as president until I return?"

Over the year that I knew Salwa, I developed a very high regard for her as a person, mother, and leader. "Of course, I will accept to act for you. It is a great honor for me."

After the call I kept wondering if I committed a fatal mistake, knowing that presidents of AUB had been kidnapped or assassinated. Fortunately, her absence was very short, less than a week. And, no major catastrophe took place during her absence.

Becoming an Amateur Painter: How it all Began

IT WAS THE END OF A VERY BUSY DAY at the American University of Beirut Medical Center (AUBMC) when the secretary of Dean Raif Nassif stopped by my office as she was leaving her office to suggest that I do something to reduce the stresses of work and the civil war.

She must have noticed on my face signs of long hours of work under very strenuous circumstances; for, in addition to my professional responsibilities in the medical school and hospital, I had responsibilities in my capacity as Associate Dean to look after the welfare of all medical students and to attend to their safety and daily needs away from their homes and families.

When I asked her for suggestions, she mentioned taking lessons in painting, and invited me to join her that evening at her painting class in the Hamaoui School of Art.

I had never painted before; the closest I came to painting was color-drawing on the blackboard, the nerve pathways of the brain during lectures to medical students.

Not to disappoint her, but seriously not interested in her suggestion, I accompanied her to the Hamaoui School of Art on Abdul Aziz Street very close to the AUB Medical Center.

It was there that evening that I met Haidar Hamaoui, the painter and teacher. The rest, as they say, is history.

What impressed me that evening, watching Haidar teach, other than his obvious artistic skill, was his humanity and humility.

Recognizing my demanding schedule, he suggested that I come to school whenever my schedule permits, not necessarily during scheduled class times. That evening marked the beginning of a long association between the two of us and our families.

I started visiting him in the school most evenings when the security situation allowed.

Haidar Hamaoui in
Hospital Bed

During our painting sessions, Haidar would paint a scene, and I would try to duplicate it as best as I could. When I finished, he would very gently suggest some alterations (retouches), to my painting.

As I advanced with my lessons, the retouch became less frequent.

An amusing snapshot of those days relates to two watercolor paintings we did in the evening. When I left the school, my painting was still wet. I left it in the school to dry and planned to pick it up the following morning on my way to work. Neither painting was signed.

When I passed by the school the next morning. I could tell from Haidar facial features that he had a story to tell. It turned out that earlier that morning, a customer passed by the school and asked Haidar if he had painted something new. Haidar showed him the two paintings, his and mine. The customer preferred mine upon which Haidar signed his name to my painting and sold it to the customer. I ended up with the master's painting.

My association with this great teacher and friend continued after we left Beirut to the USA. I made it a point every time I returned to Beirut to visit him in the school upon which time, he would introduce me to new techniques. Our close relationship continued until he passed away in February 2013 in Beirut.

My enchantment with painting also made me seek mentorship during a three-month stay in Bahrain in 1978 to 1979 with the famous Bahraini artist Abdel Karim al Bousta, whose influence is evident in my Bahraini paintings.

Finally, during a sabbatical year spent at the University of Iowa in Iowa City, I enrolled in a painting class which introduced me to Rural Iowa painting.

I attribute my enchantment with painting to the stressful work and war conditions in Lebanon in the seventies, eighties, and early nineties, to the charming and master teacher Haidar Hamaoui who made it easy for me to attend special classes with him in the time convenient to my schedule, and finally to my experience in teaching brain anatomy by illustration of the different brain tracts using different colors, a technique I learned from Dr. Malcolm Carpenter, professor of neuroanatomy at Columbia University, New York, during my residency training there in 1964-1965 and continue to practice.

Regional services

MY CLINICAL PRACTICE and teaching/research activities at AUB took me to several countries in the region for medical consultations, lectures, as an external examiner, and for research. These included visits to Palestine, Jordan, Iraq, Saudi Arabia, Kuwait, Bahrain, Sudan, Qatar, and the United Arab Emirates. Most of these were short visits except those to Palestine, Jordan, and Saudi Arabia.

Palestine

RETURN TO PALESTINE AND THE TOWN OF MY BIRTH, AKKA

> *The land I love,*
> *The playground of youth,*
> *Where passions bloom, desires glow,*
> *Whenever I remember my homeland,*
> *It reminds me of a memorable youth,*
> *Forever yearning is the eternal truth.*

From: *My Field of Play*
By Ibn al-Rumi, Poet in Baghdad during the Abbasid Caliphate

My first long trip to Palestine and my birthplace, Akka, since the Nakba was in 1987 when I was invited to talk at the Jerusalem meeting of the Palestine Psychiatric Association.

The previous trip to Palestine alluded to earlier was an overnight stop flight over Jerusalem airport on my way to Amman, Jordan to interview for a fellowship from the Royal Jordanian Army Medical Corps.

Although I was recovering from a bad back problem, I could not turn down the invitation, especially that it included a visit to my birth town, Akka, from which my family and I were displaced in 1946 and were not allowed to return by the Israeli authorities.

This visit marked the beginning of a long involvement in Palestinian education and health issues with emphasis on development, as will be detailed below.

PALESTINE THROUGH THE WELFARE ASSOCIATION (TAAWON)

I was honored to be invited to be a member of the Board of Trustees of the Welfare Association (Taawon), an association established in 1981 for the purpose of supporting developmental projects in the occupied Palestinian territories and was chair of its Programs and Projects Committee for a number of years.

As chair of the Programs and Projects Committee, I was involved in planning several health related projects in Palestine including a children's hospital in Ramallah financed by the Bahraini Chamber of Commerce, a study to link together the seven Jerusalem hospitals, and needed clinical services for children in Palestinian hospitals supported by a Saudi philanthropist.

PALESTINE THROUGH DIANA TAMARI SABBAGH FOUNDATION

As member of the Board of Trustees and chair of the cultural and education committee of the Diana Tamari Sabbagh Foundation, a foundation established by the late philanthropist Mr. Hasib Sabbagh in memory of his wife Diana Tamari Sabbagh, I had the chance to be involved in different education and health projects in Palestine.

In collaboration with a very fine group of committee members we launched several projects in Palestine including a study of the needs of the Palestinian health system conducted in collaboration with the American Public Health Association, a feasibility study for a Palestinian medical school, a sponsorship for Palestinian physicians interested in training in the USA and Canada, and a planning effort for a tertiary health center in the village of Surda in Palestine.

CHAIRING A SESSION OF THE TAAWON GENERAL ASSEMBLY

Saudi Arabia (1978-1979)

For several years, I served on the selection board of the King Faisal International Prize in Medicine, and secretary of the Board in several sessions.

For a number of years, I also taught short courses in Neuroanatomy to medical students of both the King Faisal University in Dammam and of the King Saud University students in Riad.

I joined a panel of Drs. Raymond Adams, chair of neurology in Harvard University; Dr. Fuad Sabra, chair of neurology in AUB to give a course on new developments in neurology to the ARAMCO physicians in Saudi Arabia.

Guest speakers at Aramco Medical Services, Drs. Fuad Sabra, Adel Afifi, Ray Adams

King Faisal Prize in Med Committee

THE JORDAN UNIVERSITY OF SCIENCE AND TECHNOLOGY (JUST)

In the late seventies, I was invited by Dr. Adnan Badran, President of Yarmouk University in North Jordan to be a member of the President's Advisory Board to plan the Health Science Complex in a new university in Jordan, the Jordan University of Science and Technology (JUST).

Before the structure was built, President Badran asked me to help him in placing future faculty in USA universities for doctoral training. Because of my contact with and familiarity with the University of Iowa, I arranged for all of his future faculty in the basic medical sciences to be trained at the University of Iowa, and later for a number of the clinical faculty at JUST to train at the University of Iowa. This program has succeeded beyond expectations because of the commitment to the success of the program by leaders in the college of medicine in Iowa and at JUST. At one time, there was sixty students from JUST training at the University of Iowa in the colleges of medicine, dentistry, nursing, and pharmacy.

Leaders in the College of Medicine and at JUST (Drs. Montgomery, Eckstein, Ajlouni, Abu El Haija)

THE UNIVERSITY OF JORDAN

On July 10, 1977, a Royal decree was issued to the President of the University of Jordan to appoint me as Dean of the College of Medicine at the University of Jordan. This decree was a culmination of long negotiations and several visits to Amman, Jordan to consider the invitation to assume the deanship.

My tenure as dean, however, was short. A disparity in my plans for the school, and that of some in the University leadership, made it difficult to implement my essential plans to upgrade the quality of the program.

Subsequently, I submitted my resignation to the president and returned to AUB.

Subsequent attempts by the President of the University and King Hussein of Jordan to persuade me to return were not successful.

REFUGEE FROM IRAQ

An event that I still remember during my tenure in the Deanship of Medicine of the University of Jordan was when Dr. David Hanania, a distinguished cardiac surgeon and close associate to the Royal Palace called me to ask me if I was willing to evaluate the academic qualifications of a young Iraqi physician. He was seeking refuge in Jordan claiming that he was discriminated against in Iraq and was unable to continue his research on cancer treatment. He asked Crown Prince Hasan to help him establish a cancer research institute in Amman.

I met the young man who was very well dressed, carrying a briefcase. It was apparent after a short visit that he had no academic qualifications to justify his ambitions.

Later, at the request of Prince Hasan, Dr. Hanania and I went to the Royal Palace to meet the Prince. We were surprised when we arrived at the Palace to find that the young man was present at the meeting.

Somehow, we came out with a plan to please the Prince and the young man and spare Jordan the debacle of falling in the trap of a cancer institute led by someone who was unqualified.

Subsequently Dr. Hanania, at the orders of the Prince, arranged for the young man to go to the hospital in Houston, where Dr. Hanania had his cardiology training. Years later I found that the young man had been fired from the hospital in Houston and from Harvard for misrepresentation of scientific data.

OTHER COUNTRIES

Other short visits and regional contributions included: To Iraq, as a visiting professor to survey the Baghdad University electron microscopy unit and in University of Basra to lecture in the neuroscience program; to Sudan, as visiting professor to review the neuroscience program; to Kuwait, as External Examiner in neuroscience; to Bahrain, as member of the International Committee to evaluate the School of Medicine of the Gulf University, and as a member of a team from the American University of Beirut to introduce an academic program into the Salmaniyeh Government Hospital; and to Qatar and United Arab Emirate, as a clinical consultant.

International Committee to evaluate a medical school in Bahrain

THE INDEFATIGABLE HAJJ OMAR

THE ABOVE NARRATIVE about our stay at AUB and Lebanon cannot be complete without reference to a unique person, Haj Omar Faour, Director of the AUB Transportation Department.

A man of faith who committed himself to serve the University and its family, and who took personal risks during the Lebanese civil war to ensure the smooth operation of the university and the security of its faculty and staff. I will never forget the day in 1982 he drove me in his car to purchase a battery-operated TV for Walid to watch the World Cup, on a day when the streets of Beirut were empty, and the Israeli gun boats were shelling the city. Nor will I forget the day he drove to Damascus to pick us up from the airport and back to our home in Beirut when driving on the roads was very risky because of indiscriminate shelling; or when during the civil war, he drove Rima to take her national Lebanese Baccalaureate examination and picked her up from school at the end of the exam. Or when he drove me from home to my work at AUB, and back home at the end of work for security reasons. He made it a point to check on our family when I was out of town, including providing our children with their preferred Sunday breakfast, Manakish Zaatar!

Services he provided to us were also provided to others on the faculty who needed it, always with his beautiful smile and the saying "If God wills." To ensure continued operation of the hospital during the civil war, he volunteered transport of the nurses between East and West Beirut across the dividing line, a very risky route to take.

In fact, on May 23, 1985, on one of these nurse transport missions, Haj Omar succumbed to a shrapnel injury and could not be saved.

In 1984, because of the risks of the civil war in Lebanon, we decided to accept an invitation to join the neurology department faculty of the University of Iowa with the same rank and tenure that I had held in AUB.

In retrospect, my academic career at AUB was a fulfilling career in clinical practice, teaching, research, and administration. I owe gratitude in this to many people listed elsewhere, but primarily to Dr. Raif Nassif, Dean of the School of medicine, who did not spare a moment without making sure that I got what I needed to succeed, and who was my trusted counselor and friend.

Return to USA:
Second Diaspora
(1984-)

MY FIRST DIASPORA was in 1948 from Palestine during the Nakba to Beirut, Lebanon. We left believing that the stay in Beirut would be short, only until the Arab armies retook control of Palestine. That never occurred. My parents and siblings stayed there until they passed. I went through a second diaspora in 1984 when we decided to move to the USA because the civil war in Lebanon had worsened to a degree that threatened our safety and daily living. Throughout the Lebanese civil war, I kept receiving letters and calls from Larry Anna's family in Montana, from mentors at the University of Iowa and friends in Iowa City urging us to leave Lebanon and return to the USA and Iowa City.

Of the many appreciated letters from friends and mentors, one letter that I still distinctly recall was from Dr. Rex Ingram, my neuroanatomy mentor and chair of the department of anatomy at the University of Iowa. The letter was hand-written and said:

"Dear Adel,

So far, we have been communicating mentor to mentee, but this letter is from father to son. I want you to know that you and your family are constantly in our thoughts and urge you to leave Lebanon and return to Iowa City where you are needed and loved."

Other invitations came from the New York Institute of Neurology inviting me to join the faculty.

In spite of these invitations it was difficult for us to leave Beirut until 1984, when the situation deteriorated and became unsafe. Ultimately, we decided to leave, again believing that the stay (this time in Iowa City) would be limited. The civil war lasted until 1990, by which time returning was too difficult.

Landing in the USA

Upon landing in our new diaspora, I remembered the following poem by the Umayyad Caliph Abdel Rahman, who migrated from Damascus to Spain:

"An ode to a palm tree
A palm tree stands in the middle of Rusafa,
Born in the west, far from the land of palms.
I said to it: How like me you are, far away and in exile,
In long separation from family and friends,
You have sprung from soil in which you are a stranger;
And I, like you, am far from home"

I also remembered the following poem by the Palestinian poet Mahmoud Darwish:

"We travel like everyone else,
But we return to nothing,
As if we were a path of clouds"

Carver College of Medicine

When I arrived to start work, I was asked what I desired to do: teaching, clinical work, research, or administration?

My answer: All of the above except administration!

Although my wish was, in general, respected, I could not avoid some administration. The faculty voted me to two terms on the College Executive Committee, and for one term for chair of the College Executive Committee. I accepted a request from Dr. Frank Morriss to serve as an interim Director of the Division of Child Neurology in the Department of Pediatrics from 1997 to 2001, and after my retirement I was asked by Dr. Jean Robillard, Vice President for Medical Affairs and Dean of the College of Medicine to serve as Advisor to him on the Global Health Initiative of the Carver College of Medicine from 2007 until his retirement in 2018.

Otherwise the bulk of my work was related to teaching, clinical services and research. Like students at AUB, medical students and residents at the University of Iowa liked my style of teaching and nominated me for Class teaching awards, Collegiate teaching awards, and the Regents Excellence Award.

Appreciation of my teaching and clinical practice were demonstrated by the likes of the following two notes from a student and a mother.

A student wrote

> "The journey through medical school is a difficult one, but your attention and care helped me successfully navigate through it. When I struggled, you were someone who helped me over obstacles, and when I did well, you were there to applaud my success. It is because of teachers like you that I have been able to preserve the basic tenets of humanity, kindness, compassion, and altruism with which I entered into this endeavor, and upon which I intend to build my medical career. I remain forever in your debt.

> Your skill and the grace that you display in every teaching interaction is superb. I hope that many generations of Carver College of Medicine students will be able to glean from you as much and perhaps more than I did. You believed in me and that's what made the difference.

> Thank you so much for being at once, teacher, mentor, critic, motivator, and friend."

A letter from a patient's mother read

> "Dr. Afifi was the greatest thing that ever happened to my daughter. He answered his own phone and took time to speak with us when we needed him. He is the reason she lives a full, active life now."

And a straight shooter medical student taking my course of Medical Neuroscience comments about the speed of my talking:

"Listening to Dr. Afifi's lectures is like reading the *Playboy* magazine with your wife turning the pages."

And on the lighter side, a poem from a patient:

"One made a mistake and one got right,
They said it is all from the nerves
I still have to see a hysteric
Who from hysteria was cured
Except those who visited Adel
Who treated them and their hysteria was Cured"

My Last Lecture

Between my first lecture of neuroanatomy at AUB in September 1965, and my last lecture at the Carver College of Medicine in May 2007 spanned a period of forty-seven years.

Like the first lecture, the last was also unexpectedly attended by two College dignitaries.

The topic of the lecture was a final wrap up of the Medical Neuroscience course. The speaker was scheduled to be Dr. Jean Jew. About a week before the scheduled time for the lecture, Dr. Jew asked me if I could give the lecture on her behalf, because she was tied up with other things at that time.

I happily agreed to give the lecture. Little did I know that "busy with other things" included inviting the dignitaries to attend, as well as organizing an elaborate music show by the students taking the course!

As I was waiting at the podium to start the lecture, students started coming in and settling down in their seats, as expected.

Soon, however, the scenario began to change and in came the Associate Dean for Academic Affairs, Dr. Peter Densen, followed by Dr. Terry Williams, the Chair of Anatomy, followed by two students bringing a beautiful bouquet of flowers.

As I started the lecture, from the opposite door to the lecture hall a group of students in special attire came in with their music instruments singing a song written about my teaching skills. Before I knew it, I was dragged by the students to join them with singing.

It was, to say the least, a very touching scene that I will never forget.

Somehow, I delivered the lecture and made sense of what I said.

RETIREMENT

"The art of living lies in a fine mingling of letting go and holding on"
Henry Ellis, Author, Governor of Georgia

I retired from my Carver College of Medicine responsibilities on July 1, 2007.

Several activities were planned for July 27 to make it possible for Rima and Walid and their families to arrive from Beirut and California for the occasion.

Like in the plan for my last lecture, arrangements for my retirement activities except the date were held in secret from me.

The activities for my retirement were initiated by Dr. Kathy Mathews, chair of the Division of Child Neurology in collaboration with Dr. Jeff Murray, head of Division of Genetics in the department of pediatrics, assisted by the superb organizer of the Division of Child Neurology, Melanie Devore. To all I owe gratitude and appreciation.

Several colleagues spoke in the July 27 afternoon reception held in the Damasio Conference Room of the Neurological Science Institute including Dr. Katherine Mathews, head of the Division of Child Neurology, Dr. Martin Cassel, co-Director of the Medical Neuroscience course, Dr. Daniel Bonthius, mentee and professor of child Neurology, Dr. Joseph Tamari, an old time close friend of our family and professor of Dentistry at North Western University in Chicago, Dr. Donald Brown, a mentee, Professor of Cardiology at the Carver College of Medicine, and my cardiologist. In addition, Dr. Ara Tekian, an ex-mentee of mine from AUB days and currently Associate Dean for Medical Education at the University of Illinois in Chicago came to attend the session and reception.

At the end, Walid gave a very nice talk about his experiences with me as his Dad. The session ended with me thanking the attendees and speakers.

That evening, a dinner was held in a hotel in town in which Drs. Frank Morriss, Chair of Pediatrics, Robert Rodnitzky, chair of Neurology, Melanie Devore and I spoke.

The summer 2007 issue of 'Medicine Iowa' a monthly publication of the Office of the College Dean had my photo with one of my young patients on its cover, and an article titled "A Full Life and Career."

Retirement has kept me busy. At the beginning, I told Larry Anna "from now on you will have double the husband and half the salary." After a few months of watching my retirement days, she said: "It seems I ended with no husband and half salary." She was right. Involvement in the Welfare Association (TAAWON), in the Global Health Initiative of the College, in the organization of the new Neuroscience Institute in AUB, and membership in its Board of Consultants, as well as writing my detailed memoirs for our grandchildren, co-writing two books with Dr. Ron Bergman, collating all of my paintings in one album, and digitizing all of 2x2 slides occupied my time.

One of the most pleasant highlights of retirement was the surprise celebration of our fiftieth anniversary arranged by Rima and Walid in Beirut.

Honors and Awards

UNRWA Scholar Award 1954–1957

President, Medical Students Society 1956–1957

Penrose Award for Outstanding Graduate 1957

Teacher of the Year Award, Carver College of Medicine...............1974

Certificate of Appreciation, Carver College of Medicine 1975

Teacher of the Year Award, Carver College of Medicine...............1981

Fulbright Scholar Award 1981–1982

Wilder Penfield Invited Speaker, American University of Beirut ...1984

Teaching Excellence Award...1990

Hans Zellweger Memorial Lecture Speaker...................................1990

Honorary Member, Jordan Society of Neuroscience.....................1991

Tokten (Transfer of Knowledge through Expatriate Nationals)
Award..1991

USA and Canada Representative,
Pan Arab Union of Neurological Sciences...................................1992

Appreciation Award, Jordan Pediatric Society 1995

Project Coordinator, National Plan for Human Resource
Development and Education in Palestine......................................1995–2000

Appreciation Award, Welfare Association (TAAWON) 1996, 1999

Regents Award for Faculty Excellence, University of Iowa............1997

Educator Extraordinaire, Carver College of Medicine...................1999

Appreciation Award, Palestinian Order of Physicians.....................1999

Best Doctors in the USA 1999,
2000–2004

Nominee, humanism in Medicine Award 2000

Collegiate Teaching Award 2003

Dr. Suad Sabbah Award, for the best published Scientific Work
by an American University of Beirut Alumnus 2006

Distinguished Alumnus, American University of Beirut 2011

Member, International Scientific Advisory Board Abu Haidar
Neuroscience Institute, American University of Beirut 2011–

Shuman Institute Invited Speaker..2011

Appreciation Award, Lebanese Association
for the Advancement of Science..2012

AUB Distinguished Alumnus Award with President of AUB and Dr. Nasri Kawar

At the reception of the Distinguished Alumnus Award

AUB Distinguished Alumnus Award with Larry and Dr. Nasri Kawar, chair selection committee.

SOME TESTIMONIALS

From Dr. Huda Zughbi, Internationally renowned distinguished neuroscientist:

> *"It was so wonderful seeing you and Larry during my visit. I really can't describe what an incredible influence you have had on me. I am so grateful for your mentorship and friendship."*

From Dr. Ara Tekian, Associate Dean for Education, University of Illinois, Chicago, IL:

> *"Happy birthday to my dear advisor and mentor for life, Dr. Afifi. I feel very fortunate and blessed that I have had such a distinguished mentor for decades. Without his constant encouragement, I would have never achieved the successes in my life. He is such a role model and productive that even in 2017 he published an extremely important history book about 'Medieval Islamic Medicine and Medical Luminaries' that every medical professional should have a copy"*

Post retirement at home

Wilderness of Montana

Glimpses of My Life and Career and The People Who Made Them

LIFE WILL NEVER
BE THE SAME AGAIN
NOVEMBER 26, 2016

UNLIKE OTHER SECTIONS of "Glimpses of Life and Career," I do this section with a heavy heart and deep sense of loss.

On November 26, 2016, Larry Anna passed away and with it fifty-six years of our family's happy journey together came to an end.

Her love, counsel, and support to me, the family, and whoever came in contact with her were boundless.

She joined our family as a stranger from far away land and different culture, and quickly adapted to and adopted a new culture, language, food, and idiosyncrasies.

And when she made lingual mistakes in the new language, or errors in cooking the new food, she laughed at herself and made us laugh with her.

She was more Afifi than the Afifis, more Palestinian than the Palestinians, more Lebanese than many Lebanese, and a better Muslim than many Muslims.

In times of crises, she kept her cool, kept us cool and focused, and had the incredible talent of keeping our children and their friends occupied and busy. She loved nature and made us love it as well. The dearest to her were the Rocky Mountains of the USA and Canada; places like McDonald Lake, St. Mary's Lake, Lake Louis, and Banff lakes.

Her loss was felt near and far. People in Iowa City who we did not know came to tell us how she took them under her wing when they started working with her and how she helped them develop professionally and stand on their feet. Over 115 condolence cards, e-mails, and calls were received from people who worked with her or knew her locally and abroad. An obituary prepared by the Dean of the School of Health Sciences at AUB, Dr. Iman Nuwayhid, was circulated to the AUB faculty, the AUB senate stood for a minute of silence in her memory, condolence e-mail was received by our family from Dr. Fadlo Khuri, president of AUB, an obituary appeared in the *Main Gate*, the monthly journal of AUB, and a letter of condolence was received by our family from the president of the Lebanese Order of Physicians.

We were especially touched by the support of members of the Interfaith Dialogue Group, and their families, who walked with her the difficult miles of her illness including Myrna Farraj, Nancy Hitchon, Mary Khowassah, Amal Al-Jurf among many others.

In addition, some friends touched me and supported me in my grief in a special way that I did not expect, was not familiar with, and left an impact on me. They were from different backgrounds and only related to me by friendship and collegiality, but they and their families knew Larry. They not only walked the difficult path of Larry's illness with us but continue to be with us.

Tony Traboulsi, is a highly respected attorney, highly placed in his country's political hierarchy, whom I met through a mutual friend and the two of us, and our families, became lifelong friends. I keep amusing him by telling him – 'you are my brother but from a different mother" (in Arabic: Rubaa akhin laka lam taliduhu ummak). Tony's gesture was, and continues to be, daily electronic communications that invariably include a story or joke that make me start the day smiling or laughing.

Riad Rahhal, is a colleague and fellow AUB alumnus who is on the faculty of the College of Medicine at the University of Iowa. Riad and his wife **Amal** overwhelmed us with their kindness during the last few weeks of Larry's illness, and continue their gesture by visits of Riad to our house every Sunday to have a cup of coffee with me.

John Farraj and his wife Myrna

John has been a close friend and confidant since the early sixties when we first met in Iowa City and the University of Iowa. John and I started a get together for coffee every Wednesday that has persisted until today.

Pat and Nancy Hitchon walked the miles with us. To this day, no week passes without calling and/or getting together with us.

Zuhair and Ellen Ballas

Finally, Zuhair, in spite of his very busy schedule, managed to stop by and check in as time allowed.

Dr. Don Brown with Adel

Two of the physicians who cared for her during the last stage of illness, **Dr. Gerald Jogerst** and **Dr. Donald Brown** were role models of humanistic medicine. Both walked with the family throughout her illness and Dr. Brown offered to accompany me to Mayo Clinic (in Minnesota) and stay with me through tests and procedures during a short period when neither Rima nor Walid were able to do so. Both caretakers were nominated by our family for the Carver College of Medicine 2019 Arnold Gold Humanism of Medicine Award and were judged worthy of recognition by the committee.

Dr. and Ms. Jogerst and Adel, Dr. Jogerst receiving the faculty Humanism award

The gestures of these men and women, as well as the friends who shared our loss, remind me of Charles Walcott's statement about quality of life: "The quality of a man's (person's) life is measured by how deeply he has touched the lives of others."

Two picture albums of remembrances and love were put together in her memory, one by our grandchildren Leila and Rania, and another portraying her personal and professional career of giving and love put together by the family.

Her legacy will include the many health science students she taught in AUB, Saudi Arabia, Bahrain, and the USA, and the many students from developing countries who benefited from her effort to provide opportunities for them to study at AUB.

A memorial in her name is inscribed on a rock that she loved to sit on in the Trueblood Recreation and Park area in Iowa City overlooking a lake.

SITE OF MEMORIAL FOR TETA

POSTSCRIPT

LOOKING BACK at a professional career spanning fifty-one years of teaching, research, and service, the most gratifying to me have been the following two:

1. Providing opportunities for young bright Arab health professionals for advancement. This commitment was born out of the kindness and encouragement from others gave me in the early stages of my development, and my resulting desire to "pay it forward." This instinct was reinforced by an engraving on the gate to the AUB campus that read: "That they may have life and have it more abundantly"

   A. I have always believed in the importance of a quality basic medical science education in the formation of a physician and been troubled by the paucity of qualified basic medical science faculty in regional medical schools. I had the distinct honor to lead an effort, with a group of committed colleagues at AUB, notably Dr. Samih Alami and Dr. Joseph Tamari, to provide opportunities for young professionals from regional medical schools to enroll in the AUB Basic Medical Sciences Graduate Program and return upon graduation to their institutions. This program would not have been possible without the generous donation to AUB from the Diana Tamari Sabbagh Foundation, which, not only provided support to upgrade the facilities of the AUB Basic Medical Science Graduate Program, but also to cover the cost of training of admitted applicants to the Program.

   B. I have also always believed in the importance of "man [human] before stone," the preparation of qualified human resources prior to the building of new medical schools. As a result, I enthusiastically responded in 1981 to a request from the president of the newly established Jordan University of Science and Technology (JUST) Dr. Adnan Badran, to assist in the training of their future faculty. This was the beginning of a long-term relationship discussed earlier between the University of Iowa and Jordan University of Science and Technology (JUST). Since its inception, over sixty Jordanian faculty members from JUST have trained at the University of Iowa then returned to the colleges of medicine, dentistry, nursing, and pharmacy in Jordan. Some of the Iowa graduates assumed leadership positions in their colleges, including chairmanships and deans. One alumnus of this program (with training in nursing) even became a minister in the Jordanian cabinet. This program could not have been achieved or succeeded without the support of visionary leaders of the Jordan University of Science and Technology, namely President Adnan Badran, and the global perspective of health education by the leaders at the College of Medicine such as Dean John Eckstein, Associate Dean Rex Montgomery, Vice President for Medical Affairs Dr. Jean Robillard, and their counterparts in the colleges of Dentistry, pharmacy, and Nursing at the University of Iowa.

C.   The success of the global health program between the University of Iowa and JUST encouraged me, in collaboration with Vice President Jean Robillard, to duplicate it at the request of Dr. Kamal Badr, the visionary Dean of a new medical school at the Lebanese American University (LAU), in Beirut, Lebanon. Following an encouraging beginning in which the University of Iowa provided opportunities for students from LAU to spend time in research laboratories at the University of Iowa, training the LAU professor of anatomy, assistance in recruitment of their faculty and in designing their courses in gross anatomy and neuroscience, as well as introducing to them the virtual anatomy program used at the University of Iowa, the project had to be discontinued because of the resignation of two LAU deans.

2. Responding to the needs of the health sector (health education institutions and health services) in the occupied Palestinian territories (OPT) to achieve the quality of health education and services they aspire to.

   A. With support of a group of committed colleagues from the American University of Beirut faculty of medicine, and with generous financial support from the Diana Tamari Sabbagh Foundation, I was fortunate to lead an effort in the early eighties (in collaboration with the American Public Health Association) to map out the needs of the health sector in Palestinian territories under occupation.

   B. Working with colleagues from RAND Corporation in Washington DC, an updated report was developed to map out priority needs of the health sector in the first ten years of the new state of Palestine.

   C. Along the same theme, I had the honor to lead an international group of health education experts in conducting a feasibility study for a Palestinian Medical School.

   D. Through my membership in the Welfare Association Board of Trustees and, especially as Chair of the Project and Program Committee, I had the opportunity to channel necessary funding to the health and education sectors in the Occupied Palestinian Territories (OPT). Among the programs supported through these efforts were: The Children's Hospital in Ramallah, a children's oncology unit at Augusta Victoria Hospital in Jerusalem, and the pediatric cardiac surgery and pathology units at al- Makassed Hospital in Jerusalem. We also assisted in the establishment of a National Center for Child Development and Disabilities at al-Najah University.

Glimpses of My Life and Career and The People Who Made Them

Then and Now:
A Retrospective Look at Fifty Years of Teaching, Patient Care, and Research

AS I REFLECT BACK on 50 years of teaching, patient care and research, several contrasts come to mind between when I started medicine and what medicine has become.

TEACHING

THEN: Medicine was a calling.

NOW: Medicine has become a business.

THEN: Students were taught about prevention and relief of suffering.

NOW: Students hear more of "throughput, capture of market, units of service, and the bottom line."

THEN: Lecture halls were packed with motivated students.

NOW: They are barely a quarter full of students following handouts or checking their cell phones.

THEN: Teachers told students what they needed to know.

NOW: Teachers are told by students what they (students) need to learn.

THEN: Teachers were expected to teach students.

NOW: They are expected to please them.

THEN: Teachers improvised during lecture.

NOW: They are expected to stick to the handouts.

TEACHING

THEN: Teachers strove to educate and motivate students.

NOW: They facilitate their passing national exams.

THEN: Students asked challenging and thought-provoking questions.

NOW: They ask what they need to know to pass the examination.

THEN: Students bought required textbooks and read required assignments.

NOW: They diligently read detailed handouts.

THEN: College leadership took pride in the quality of students.

NOW: They take pride in the percentage passing national exams.

THEN: Teachers' main objective was to teach.

NOW: It is to win teaching awards.

THEN: Students' feet were placed on the floor of the lecture hall where they belong.

NOW: They are up on the chair in front and in the teacher's face.

THEN: Students came to the lecture hall and stayed through the lecture.

NOW: They come to set their recorder and leave.

THEN: The topic of the lecture was the impetus for students and residents to attend noon conferences.

NOW: It is the provided lunch.

THEN: Time spent by residents in the hospital was determined by their patients' needs and the resident educational objectives.

NOW: It is legislated by a set of arbitrary number of hours based on an aberration in big cities emergency rooms.

Glimpses of My Life and Career and The People Who Made Them

CLINICAL SERVICE

THEN: Patients entered the examination room from the same door as the physician and nurses.

NOW: Patients enter the examination room from a separate door than that assigned for doctors and nurses.

THEN: Health care professionals thought through the clinical history, physical examination, and laboratory results, and made final judgment on the best course of action.

NOW: Corporate culture thinks for you. Your role is to implement management protocols, standards of practice protocols etc.

THEN: Night calls were a given for practicing physicians whether for private practice or academic medicine.

NOW: Night calls for academic physicians are to be avoided in any way possible.

THEN: Health professionals' mission was to heal.

NOW: The mission is to document.

THEN: The text of letters to the referring physicians was intended to convey relative information.

NOW: It is designed by a committee to retrieve maximum payments from insurance companies.

THEN: Clinicians' summaries of visits were meant to document quality medical care.

NOW: The summaries are designed to ensure adequate reimbursements.

THEN: The physician faced the patient during history taking and examination.

NOW: The physician faces a computer screen through most of the visit.

THEN: We decided when it is appropriate to answer our pager.

NOW: It is determined for us by a hospital executive who never answered a pager.

THEN: A physician was a highly respected member of the community.

NOW: Physicians' respect is declining.

CLINICAL SERVICE

THEN: Faculty member value to the institution was measured by his/her competence, academic contributions, and esteem of colleagues.

NOW: It is determined by how many Relative Value Units (RVU) he/she accumulates.

THEN: Teaching contributions were measured based on quality.

NOW: They are measured by an arbitrary numerical scale set by the administration.

THEN: Teaching of students and residents was viewed as a privilege.

NOW: It is looked at as a chore and a diversion from the more important research and /or service, an attitude that can easily rub off from one generation to the next.

THEN: We attended conferences to learn.

NOW: We attend conferences to gather points for licensure.

THEN: Faculty were entrusted with how they spend their time in the office.

NOW: They have to fill faculty time studies bi-annually for two weeks of work, in half hour daily segments.

THEN: Membership on committees was based on merit.

NOW: It is to buttress the promotion dossier.

THEN: Office environment was friendly and cordial.

NOW: It is dominated by rules and regulations.

THEN: Practicing physicians were called healers.

NOW: They are health providers.

THEN: We talked about the healing arts.

NOW: We talk about health care industry.

THEN: We treated patients, and their families.

NOW: We treat clients, customers, and consumers.

THEN: The leaders of academic units were called chairs or heads of the unit.

NOW: They are Chief Executive Officers (CEO) as in business companies.

Samih (Afifi) and Adel (Alami)

Glimpses of My Life and Career and The People Who Made Them

An Ode to Samih Alami

"GLIMPSES OF LIFE AND CAREER" will not be complete without reference to Dr. Samih Alami, a colleague, friend, counselor for over fifty years. We were so close that friends called him Samih Afifi and called me Adel Alami.

We first met at AUB, both of us Palestinian refugees, he from Gaza, and I from Akka, and very soon built a strong bond of friendship until he died prematurely from a disease he knew so much about.

A panorama of memories, happy and not so happy, unfolded at the news of his loss. Memories of classrooms and classmates, the AUB soda fountain, campus walks, the hearts he touched, loved, or broke, evenings spent together by the seaside chatting, the innocent look on his face as he handed me the keys to his apartment to take him back and tuck him in, working together in al-Urwat al Wuthqa Society and the Civic Welfare League, or going for coffee or lunch at Faisal restaurant across the main gate or at his brother Sami's home, or our home. We were basically inseparable.

Samih and I shared many attributes and interests. Both of us were obsessed with working to improve Palestinian educational institutions and the provision of opportunities for bright Palestinian students to access higher educational institutions abroad.

He single-handedly started the Palestine students aid fund which expanded later by donations from philanthropists and governments.

Glimpses of My Life and Career and The People Who Made Them

Concluding Thoughts

LOOKING BACK AT MY JOURNEY, it became obvious how fortunate I was to have parents and family friends who valued education for their children. They used their own diminishing resources following the Nakba in Palestine to support my education. This was a risky proposition for everyone under the prevailing circumstances after the Nakba, since the return on their investment was not guaranteed.

Fortunately, however, the investments paid off beyond my and their expectations. The support I subsequently received from AUB, and from Arab and international foundations resulted in multiplying many fold the initial investment and touching multiple other deserving young beneficiaries.

Looking back at the record of achievement I was fortunate to accumulate, I recognize it as a reflection of the many individual men and women, and Foundations who believed in the value of education. They are deserving of utmost credit which motivated me to develop this document, and to reflect the mission of the AUB Founders which is inscribed on the AUB Main Gate: **'That they may have life and have it more abundantly.'**

Glimpses of My Life and Career and The People Who Made Them

Epilogue:
More Memorable Glimpses

Chatting with Dr. Fuad Haddad prior to delivering the Wilder Penfield Memorial Lecture

Larry with some of the Department faculty

Larry Anna visit to the Human Morphology Department at AUB

Daily get together with Dr. Samih Alami in his office in the AUB Hospital

My parents in the garden of their favorite summer resort hotel in Hamanna, Lebanon

Celebrating the centennial anniversary
of the Department of Neurology
in the Carver College of Medicine.
Recognizing faculty members who
left a legacy

College Classmates at AUB

Glimpses of My Life and Career and The People Who Made Them

At the Jabbur's compound in Nabak, Syria

*Overnight rest
stop in a Danish
missionary hospital
on our way to
conduct research
on the crania
of Syrian desert
Bedouins*

*With Drs. Ron Bergman
and Garry Van Hosen,
colleagues in the
Department of Anatomy,
Carver College of
Medicine, University of
Iowa*

*Medical students, Carver
College of Medicine,
celebrating the end of the
Medical Neuroscience
Course*

Part of the students show celebrating the end of the neuroscience course with the title of the song they sang

My photo hanging in the library/conference room of the Department of Human Morphology commemorating my department leadership from 1969-1985

Conducting feasibility study for a Palestinian Medical School

Child Neurology faculty, Carver College of Medicine, University of Iowa

Glimpses of My Life and Career and The People Who Made Them

With Ron Bergman, Bill and Marilyn Osborne, colleagues and friends in Iowa City

Displaying two books co-authored with Dr. Ron Berman in the atrium of the Department of Anatomy, Carver College of Medicine, University of Iowa

Graduation of Rima celebrated by us and grandparents Pattens, 1987

Caricature created by Caven, a medical student in AUB in 1979 depicting inseparable link to my pipe at that time

Distinguished faculty and staff of the Department of Human Morphology who together established the first modern department of anatomy and coined the name Department of Human Morphology

Made in United States
North Haven, CT
09 November 2021

10976654R00062

ISBN 9780578637709